THE BICYCLE MAN
by Allen Say

Center for the Collaborative Classroom

This Center for the Collaborative Classroom edition is published by
arrangement with Houghton Mifflin Harcourt Publishing Company.

Center for the Collaborative Classroom
1001 Marina Village Parkway, Suite 110
Alameda, CA 94501
800.666.7270 ★ fax: 510.464.3670
collaborativeclassroom.org

ISBN 978-1-61003-189-9

Printed in China

5 6 7 8 9 10 RRD 20 19 18

For Morita Sensei

When I was a small boy I went to a school in the south island of Japan. The schoolhouse stood halfway up a tall green mountain. It was made of wood and the wood was gray with age. When a strong wind blew, the trees made the sound of waves and the building creaked like an old sailing ship. From the playground we could see the town, the ships in the harbor, the shining sea.

One fine spring day we had our sportsday. All the children and teachers were out in the playground long before the first bell rang.

"Did everybody remember to bring a headband?" asked Mrs. Morita. She was our first-grade teacher. Eagerly we showed her our headbands. They were red on one side and white on the other. "Remember, we're on the red team," she told us.

8

We swept the playground with all the brooms in the school. We tied colored flags and streamers to bamboo poles. We drew white lines on the ground with powdered chalk.

Our parents came carrying tiered lunch boxes and kettles filled with tea. They spread their straw mats and sat around the oval track.

When everything was ready Mrs. Morita rang the bell. It was nine o'clock. The principal stood on the platform and said, "Parents, children, my fellow teachers, let us remember that we are gathered here in the spirit of sportsmanship. Whether we win or lose, let us enjoy ourselves."

We cheered and clapped our hands.

The youngest children were the first to race. We lined up six at a time at the starting line.

"Ready, set, go!" Mr. Oka, the art teacher, boomed at us. We first graders leaped out and dashed around the track. Parents and teachers ran alongside of us, yelling encouragement. The older children waved flags and headbands and shouted at the top of their lungs until the mountain echoed the noise like rumbling thunder.

The winners went up to the judges' table and received prizes from the principal. The prizes were wrapped in white paper and tied with gold threads. Inside, there were oranges and rice cakes and pencils.

By the time the sixth graders finished running it was lunchtime. And that was the best part of the sportsday. My mother had cooked for two days preparing the good things to eat. The layers of lacquered boxes held pickled melon rinds and egg rolls, spiced rice and fish cakes. There were apples and peaches and sweets of all sorts.

In the afternoon we had the tug of war and piggyback races.
After that the grown-ups had a race of their own. Parents and

teachers paired up and tied their ankles together with headbands and hopped around the oval. We screamed with delight when they stumbled and fell on top of one another.

We were cheering Mrs. Morita and someone's father when a hush fell on the playground. We stopped moving and talking and stared toward the gate.

Two strangers were leaning over the fence and watching us. They were American soldiers. One of them was a white man with bright hair like fire, and the other man had a face as black as the earth. They wore dark uniforms with neckties, soft caps on their heads, and red stripes on their sleeves. They had no guns.

"Look how black he is!"

"Look at the red hair!" we whispered.

The war had been over for only a short while, not even one year. American soldiers had a base in the harbor but we had never seen them in our mountain. I felt afraid.

21

The foreigners smiled and waved at us. When the black man cleared the fence and came toward us we all drew back and stared. He was the tallest man I had ever seen. And his clothes! Such sharp creases! And his shoes shone like polished metal.

The soldier walked in huge strides toward the school entrance where the principal's bicycle stood. He pointed at the bicycle and turned to the judges' table. The principal stood up slowly.

"He wants the bicycle," someone said.

"Maybe he doesn't know what it is."

"No, he wants to ride it."

The principal walked up to the American and bowed. He looked like a small boy greeting a giant. The tall man gave a deep bow, almost bumping heads with the principal. We started to giggle.

We watched them talk to each other with their hands. The principal pointed at the bicycle, then at the man, and nodded. Yes, you are welcome to ride my bicycle, he seemed to say. The soldier put the palms of his hands together and smiled.

The man took the bicycle by the handlebar, kicked up the stand, and rolled it out to the center of the playground. He motioned to us to make room, and then called his friend.

The other American was nearly as tall as the black man. He took off his cap and saluted us with a big bow. We giggled and bowed back. The strangers spoke to each other and nodded.

The black man took off his jacket and handed it to the white man. Then he hoisted a long leg over the bicycle and began to pedal it round and round in a widening circle. His friend waved the jacket like a flag and cheered him to go faster.

Suddenly the rider yanked on the handlebar and lifted the front
wheel off the ground.

"Oh, look!" we stirred.

"How can he ride like that?"

"What an athlete!" said the art teacher.

The red-haired man was the ringmaster. He ran alongside of the bicycle and shouted encouragement. The rider went round and round, with only one wheel, zigzagging this way and that. We were amazed.

Then he rode backwards!

He sat on the bicycle with his body turned around. He had to twist his neck to see where he was going. He worked his long arms and legs like a huge dancing spider. We howled with wonder.

The man rode backwards, then forwards, twirling the front wheel like a spinning gyroscope. He shouted something to the ringmaster who grasped the carrier and began to push as fast as

he could. Then he let go.

The bicycle shot forward with great speed. The rider stood up on the pedals and, leaning on the handlebar, put both his feet up

on the carrier! He was in the air. His cap flew off and his necktie
fluttered in the wind. He seemed to be flying free, cruising like an
enormous dragonfly. "Oh, oh!" we exclaimed and gasped in turn.

When the bicycle finally came to a stop the playground roared with wild clapping of hands and shouting. The rider panted, heaving and laughing. The ringmaster rushed up to him and lifted him in a bear hug. We mobbed around them, jumping and yelling.

The principal struggled through the crowd and the black man reached out to him. They gripped each other's arms like old friends.

The principal raised his arms to quiet us down. He took the soldiers' hands and led them to the platform. There he whispered something to Mrs. Morita and she brought him the largest box from the prize table.

The principal stood on the platform and held out the box to the Americans. He looked like the emperor awarding a great champion.

The bicycle rider received the gift with both hands and lifted it high above his head. Then he turned to the crowd.

39

"Ari-ga-tow, ari-ga-tow," he said. "Thank you, thank you." The whole school bowed to him, and shouted for joy.

The Americans put their caps on and walked out the gate with their prize. They went down the mountain, arm in arm, waving and laughing. We followed them with our eyes, until they disappeared around the bend in the road.

41

The Center for the Collaborative Classroom (CCC) is a nonprofit organization dedicated to students' growth as critical thinkers who learn from, care for, and respect one another. Since 1980, we have created innovative curricula and provided continuous professional learning that empower teachers to transform classrooms, build school community, and inspire the academic and social growth of children.

Authentic literature is at the heart of our literacy programs. Children's books are deeply interwoven into every lesson, either in a read-aloud or as part of individual student work. Rich, multicultural fiction and nonfiction bring the full range of human experience and knowledge into the classroom, reinforce students' sense of belonging within it, and connect the classroom to the wider world.

Engaged teachers facilitate the exchange of student ideas in collaborative classrooms. These conversations spark curiosity and a desire to participate in the learning process that reap benefits far beyond the immediate goals of learning to read and write. Combining quality curricula and great literature enriches the educational experience for all students and teachers.

We would like to express our thanks to Houghton Mifflin Harcourt Publishing Company for allowing us to reprint this book.